D0758050

COOL CATS

Birmans

by Christina Leaf

BELLWETHER MEDIA • MINNEAPOLIS, MN

Note to Librarians, Teachers, and Parents:

Blastoff! Readers are carefully developed by literacy experts and combine standards-based content with developmentally appropriate text.

Level 1 provides the most support through repetition of high-frequency words, light text, predictable sentence patterns, and strong visual support.

Level 2 offers early readers a bit more challenge through varied simple sentences, increased text load, and less repetition of high-frequency words.

Level 3 advances early-fluent readers toward fluency through increased text and concept load, less reliance on visuals, longer sentences, and more literary language.

Level 4 builds reading stamina by providing more text per page, increased use of punctuation, greater variation in sentence patterns, and increasingly challenging vocabulary.

Level 5 encourages children to move from "learning to read" to "reading to learn" by providing even more text, varied writing styles, and less familiar topics.

Whichever book is right for your reader, Blastoff! Readers are the perfect books to build confidence and encourage a love of reading that will last a lifetime!

This edition first published in 2016 by Bellwether Media, Inc.

No part of this publication may be reproduced in whole or in part without written permission of the publisher. For information regarding permission, write to Bellwether Media, Inc., Attention: Permissions Department, 5357 Penn Avenue South, Minneapolis, MN 55419.

Library of Congress Cataloging-in-Publication Data

Leaf, Christina, author.
  Birmans / by Christina Leaf.
    pages cm. – (Blastoff! Readers. Cool Cats)
  Summary: "Relevant images match informative text in this introduction to Birman cats. Intended for students in kindergarten through third grade"– Provided by publisher.
  Audience: Ages 5-8
  Audience: K to grade 3
  Includes bibliographical references and index.
  ISBN 978-1-62617-231-9 (hardcover: alk. paper)
  1. Birman cat–Juvenile literature. 2. Longhair cats–Juvenile literature. 3. Cat breeds–Juvenile literature. I. Title.
  SF449.B5L43 2016
  636.8'3–dc23
                    2015005081

33614059673953

Table of Contents

What Are Birmans?

Birmans are a gentle cat **breed**.

4

These loving pets like to be held.

They are semi-longhaired cats with beautiful, soft **coats**.

Their paws look like
white mittens.

France

Burma
(Myanmar)

N
W   E
S

Birmans are known as the **Sacred** Cats of Burma. They once lived in **temples** with **priests**.

In the early 1900s, a pair of Birmans set sail for France from Asia. The female gave birth to kittens when she arrived in France.

More cats were **bred** from the litter. They quickly became popular in Europe.

Birmans arrived in the United States in 1959. Now they are favorite pets in the U.S.!

Birmans are medium-sized cats. They have **stocky** bodies and short legs. Their heads are round. Fluffy **ruffs** circle their necks.

Birman Profile

— blue eyes

— neck ruff

— white paws

Weight: 6 to 15 pounds (3 to 7 kilograms)

Life Span: 12 to 16 years

Birmans have **silky** fur.
As kittens, they are all white.

Adults have **point coats**. They are light-colored with darker fur on the face, ears, legs, and tail.

There are many colors of Birmans. They include chocolate and **lilac**.

Birman Coats

chocolate

lilac

cream

seal

All Birmans have white paws and blue eyes.

Calm and Social

Birmans are calm and quiet. They call for attention with soft chirps.

Most Birmans spend their time
relaxing around the house.
But many enjoy playing.

Birmans get lonely by themselves.
These social cats like being with
people and other pets.

They want to help with anything their owners are doing. Many even greet their owners at the door!

Glossary

bred—purposely mated two cats to make kittens with certain qualities

breed—a type of cat

coats—the hair or fur covering some animals

lilac—a light gray color

point coats—light-colored coats with darker fur in certain areas; pointed cats have dark faces, ears, legs, and tails.

priests—religious leaders

ruffs—areas of longer fur around the necks of some animals

sacred—highly respected and honored

silky—soft, smooth, and shiny

stocky—thick in build

temples—religious buildings

To Learn More

AT THE LIBRARY

Miller, Connie Colwell. *Birman Cats*. Mankato, Minn.: Capstone Press, 2009.

Petrie, Kristin. *Birman Cats*. Minneapolis, Minn.: ABDO Publishing Company, 2014.

Sexton, Colleen. *The Life Cycle of a Cat*. Minneapolis, Minn.: Bellwether Media, 2011.

ON THE WEB

Learning more about Birmans is as easy as 1, 2, 3.

1. Go to www.factsurfer.com.

2. Enter "Birmans" into the search box.

3. Click the "Surf" button and you will see a list of related web sites.

With factsurfer.com, finding more information is just a click away.

Index

The images in this book are reproduced through the courtesy of: Eric Isselee, front cover, pp. 4, 7, 13, 17 (top right, bottom left, bottom right), 21; Juniors Bildarchiv/ Superstock/ Alamy/ Glow Images, pp. 5, 12, 14, 15, 16; Labat-Rouquette/ Kimball Stock, p. 6; Jean Michel Ardea/ Labat/ Animals Animals, pp. 9, 20; P. Wegner/ Glow Images, p. 10; Angela Hampton Picture Library/ Alamy, p. 11; Linn Currie, p. 17 (top left); absolutimages, p. 18; Tierfotoagentur/ Alamy, p. 19.